TAR

WORSHIP TOGETHER® PLATINUM

ISBN 0-634-09918-3

HAL•LEONARD® CORPORATION
7777 W. BLUEMOUND RD. P.O. BOX 13819 MILWAUKEE, WI 53213

Visit Hal Leonard Online at
www.halleonard.com

BE GLORIFIED

Words and Music by LOUIE GIGLIO,
CHRIS TOMLIN and JESSE REEVES

BETTER IS ONE DAY

Words and Music by
MATT REDMAN

BLESSED BE YOUR NAME

Words and Music by MATT REDMAN
and BETH REDMAN

Recorded a half step lower.

BREATHE

Words and Music by
MARIE BARNETT

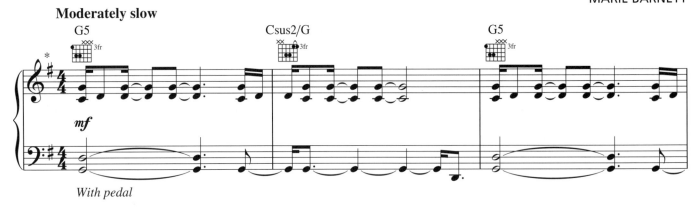

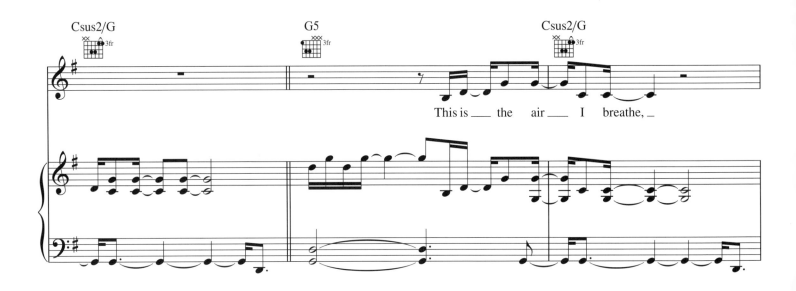

This is ___ the air ___ I breathe, ___

this is ___ the air ___ I breathe, ___ Your ho - ly pres-

Recorded a half step lower.

DRAW ME CLOSE

Words and Music by
KELLY CARPENTER

THE HAPPY SONG

Words and Music by
MARTIN SMITH

Oh, I could sing un - end - ing

I could sing dance a thou - sand

Solo ends

cel - e - brate, hey, for joy is in ___ this

place. *Vocal 1st time only*
Instrumental solo - ad lib.

1,3

2,4

Oh, ___ I could sing un -

Solo ends

ENOUGH

Words and Music by CHRIS TOMLIN
and LOUIE GIGLIO

Moderate Rock

You are my __ sup - ply, __ my breath __ of __ life. __
You're my sac - ri - fice __ of great - est __ price. __

__ Still more awe - some than I __ know. __   You are my __ re - ward, __
__ Still more awe - some than I __ know. __   You're my com - ing __ king. __

EVERY MOVE I MAKE

Words and Music by
DAVID RUIS

FOREVER

Words and Music by
CHRIS TOMLIN

Give thanks to the Lord, ___ our
With a might - y hand and
From the ris - ing to the

God and ___ King. ___ His love en - dures ___ for - ev -
out - stretched arm, ___ His love en - dures ___ for - ev -
set - ting ___ sun, ___ His love en - dures ___ for - ev -

- er.
- er. For He is good, ___ He is a -
- er. And by the grace of ___ God ___ we will
For the life ___ that's

HE REIGNS

Words and Music by PETER FURLER
and STEVE TAYLOR

THE HEART OF WORSHIP

Words and Music by
MATT REDMAN

HERE I AM TO WORSHIP

Words and Music by
TIM HUGHES

Moderately slow

Light of the World, You stepped down in-to dark - ness,
King of all days, oh so high - ly ex - alt - ed,

o - pened my eyes, let me ___ see. ___ Beau - ty that made this ___
glo - rious in heav - en a - bove. ___ Hum - bly You came to the

heart a - dore ___ You, hope of a life spent with ___ You. ___)
earth You cre - a - ted, all for love's sake be - came ___ poor. ___)

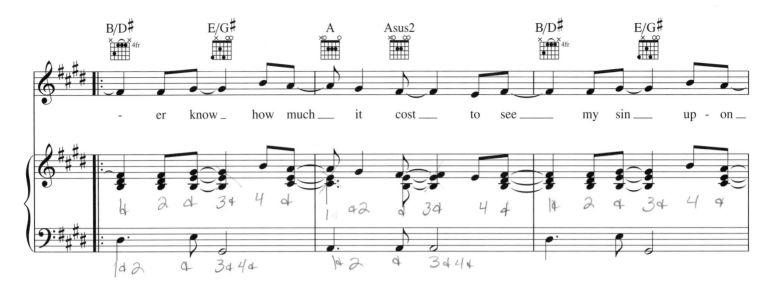

-er know_ how much___ it cost___ to see_____ my sin___ up - on___

___ that cross.__ And I'll nev - ___ that cross.__ Here I am to

D.S. al Coda

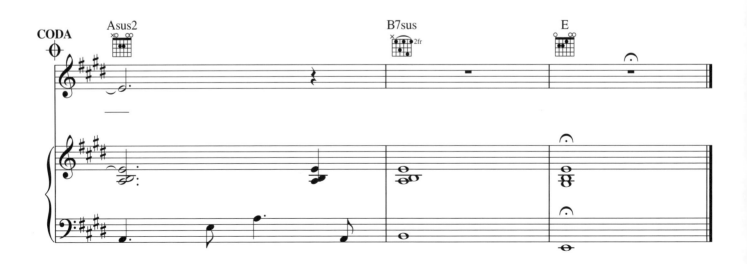

I COULD SING OF YOUR LOVE FOREVER

Words and Music by
MARTIN SMITH

HOLY IS THE LORD

Words and Music by CHRIS TOMLIN
and LOUIE GIGLIO

I WANT TO KNOW YOU
(In the Secret)

Words and Music by
ANDY PARK

IT IS YOU

Words and Music by
PETER FURLER

As we lift up our hands, ___ will You meet us here? ___ As we call on Your name, _

___ will You meet us here? ___ We have come to this place ___ to wor-ship You, _

___ God of mer-cy and grace. ___ It is You ___ we a-dore. _

LET EVERYTHING THAT HAS BREATH

Words and Music by
MATT REDMAN

LORD, REIGN IN ME

Words and Music by
BRENTON BROWN

LORD, I LIFT YOUR NAME ON HIGH

Words and Music by
RICK FOUNDS

Lord, I lift Your name __ on high.

Lord, I love to sing __ Your prais - es.

O PRAISE HIM
(All This for a King)

Words and Music by
DAVID CROWDER

SONG OF LOVE

Words and Music by REBECCA ST. JAMES,
MATT BRONLEEWE and JEREMY ASH

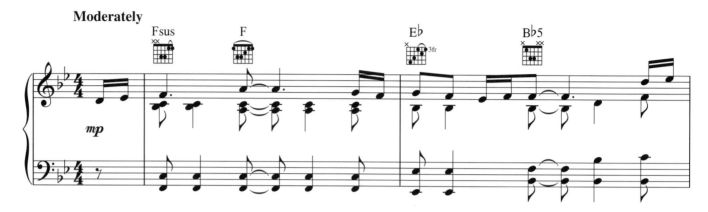

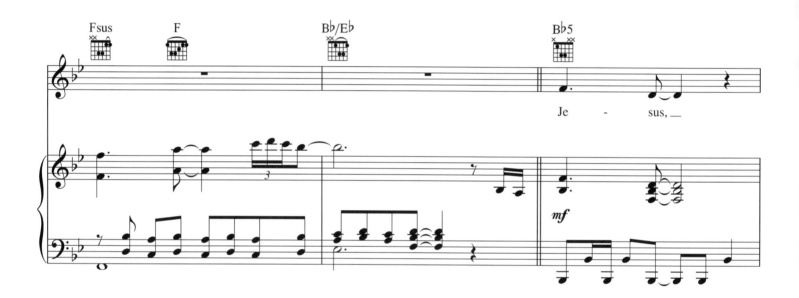

Original key: B major. This edition has been transposed down one half-step to be more playable.

THE WONDERFUL CROSS

Words and Music by JESSE REEVES,
CHRIS TOMLIN and J.D. WALT

When I sur-vey the won-drous
See from His head, His hands, His
Were the whole realm of na-ture

cross on which the Prince of Glo-ry
feet, sor-row and love flow min-gled
mine, that were an of-f'ring far too

died, my rich-est gain I count but
down. Did e'er such love and sor-row
small. Love so a-maz-ing, so di-